AF596793

# KARMA'S TAPESTRY

## WEAVING A LIFE OF SELFLESS SERVICE

DR. MINAKSHI BANSAL

Made with ♥ on the Notion Press Platform
www.notionpress.com

## *DEDICATION*

***This book is dedicated to all who find joy and purpose in the service of others—to the volunteers, caregivers, educators, and every unsung hero whose quiet acts of kindness weave the fabric of our shared humanity. May this book inspire you to continue your journey of selfless service, knowing that your contributions ripple across time and space, crafting a legacy of compassion and connection.***

♡♡♡

# Contents

# Contents

# Prayer

*"Om Poornamadah Poornamidam Poornaat Poornamudachyate, Poornasya Poornamaadaya Poornamevavashishyate"*

*"Om Shantih, Shantih, Shantih"*

*The literal interpretation of this mantra is: That which is Absolute, This which is Absolute, Absolute arises from Absolute, If Absolute is removed from Absolute, Absolute remains*

*This mantra is a reminder of the fundamental truth that all of existence is rooted in the Absolute. It is a reminder that the Absolute is the source of all that is, and that it is ever-present, even when all else is taken away. It is a reminder of the peace that comes from understanding and accepting this truth.*

*Om Peace, Peace, Peace.*

# About The Author

Dr. Minakshi Bansal, born in the bustling metropolis of Delhi, India, has led a life steeped in artistry, scholarly pursuit, and an unwavering commitment to societal betterment. Following her marriage, she relocated to Ahmedabad, Gujarat, where she has since blossomed into a multifaceted beacon of inspiration for many. Dr. Minakshi is not only recognized as a gifted artist in the realm of Fine Arts but also as an esteemed author, a devoted social worker and a dedicated research scholar in Psychology. Her journey, marked by a profound dedication to elevating those around her, especially the downtrodden and underprivileged children of society, is a testament to her deep-seated belief in the transformative power of engagement and empathy.

From her earliest days, Minakshi was distinguished by an insatiable appetite for reading. Her literary universe was inhabited by characters and narratives that spanned ethical tales, motivational and inspirational stories, and the mythic parables imbued with life lessons. This voracious reading habit was not merely for personal edification but was driven by a desire to distill and disseminate the essence of these narratives to foster the development of students and peers alike. She was particularly captivated by the lives and teachings of historical figures and spiritual leaders such as Adi Shankaracharya, Swami Vivekananda, Dr. APJ Abdul Kalam, Mahamana Pandit Madan Mohan Malviya, Mahatma Gandhi, Sardar Vallabhai Patel, and Vinoba Bhave, among others. Their philosophies and life stories fueled her ambition to embody their ideals of resilience, selflessness, and relentless pursuit of knowledge.

Dr. Minakshi's academic and practical engagement with psychology has been equally noteworthy. As a research scholar, her focus has been on exploring the intricate tapestry of the human psyche, aiming to unlock the potential for psychological well-being and societal harmony. Her scholarly work is complemented by her active involvement in social work, where she employs her academic insights to make tangible differences in the lives of the underprivileged. Her endeavours in social work are characterized by an innovative approach that combines traditional wisdom with contemporary psychological practices to address the multifaceted challenges faced by these communities.

Her artistic talents, another facet of her diverse capabilities, are not merely a personal passion but also serve as a medium through which she communicates and connects with others. Her art, rich in symbolism and emotional depth, reflects her philosophical inquiries and social concerns, offering viewers a glimpse into the breadth of her intellect and the depth of her compassion.

In addition to her contributions to the arts and social sciences, Dr. Minakshi has embraced the healing arts of Pranic Healing, mastering the techniques developed by Master Choa Kok Sui. This practice, which focuses on the manipulation of Prana or life energy to heal the body and aura, has been both a personal journey of discovery and a means through which she extends her healing touch to others. Her proficiency in Pranic Healing is complemented by her advocacy and teaching of various forms of meditation aimed at rejuvenation, personal betterment, and the cultivation of harmony within individuals and communities alike.

Dr. Minakshi's life is a narrative of relentless pursuit, not just of personal achievement but of the upliftment and empowerment of society at large. Her diverse interests and talents—spanning the arts, literature, psychology, and the healing practices—converge on a singular path of service. She embodies the spirit of the luminaries who inspired her, channelling their legacy through her actions and teachings. Through her books, art, and social initiatives, she continues to inspire a new generation to embark on their own journeys of self-discovery, resilience, and altruism.

Her commitment to social betterment, particularly her focus on uplifting underprivileged children, reflects a deep understanding of the transformative potential of education and personal development. By integrating her knowledge of psychology, her artistic sensibilities, and her healing practices, Dr. Bansal has developed a holistic approach to social work that addresses both the immediate needs and the long-term well-being of the communities she serves.

As an author, Dr. Minakshi's writings offer a blend of inspirational insights, practical wisdom, and reflective contemplations drawn from her extensive reading and life experiences. Her books serve as a guide for those seeking to navigate the complexities of life with grace, resilience, and purpose. Through her narratives, she extends an invitation to her readers to explore the depths of their own potential and to contribute meaningfully to the collective well-being of society.

In Dr. Minakshi Bansal, we find a remarkable synthesis of the artist, the scholar, the healer, and the social activist. Her life's work stands as a beacon of hope and a source of inspiration for individuals seeking to make a difference in the world. Her story is a compelling reminder of the power of individual action, rooted in compassion and driven by a profound commitment to the betterment of humanity. Dr. Minakshi's legacy is not just in the tangible outcomes of her efforts but in the enduring spirit of inquiry, empathy, and service that she embodies.

# Preface

Service to others—selfless, unwavering, and compassionate—is the golden thread that binds the fabric of humanity. In this book, we explore the profound implications of leading a life dedicated to helping others, not merely as an act but as a transformative journey that enriches the giver as much as, if not more than, the receiver. The essence of selfless service, or what we might term as karma in its purest form, is a pathway to discovering deeper meanings and connections in our lives. Through this exploration, we uncover how each act of kindness and every moment of giving stitches together a vast, intricate tapestry of human experience and emotion.

Service is often seen as an outward act directed at others, but its true impact is much more profound and personal. The narratives shared in this book delve into this inner transformation, illuminating how the act of giving can lead to significant personal growth and fulfillment. These stories and reflections offer a window into the journeys of individuals who have found their purpose and passion in serving others, showcasing the diverse ways in which service can manifest and the myriad paths it can take.

This exploration is grounded in the belief that everyone has something valuable to offer, and that the act of service is not confined to grand gestures or monumental commitments. Rather, it is found in the everyday acts of kindness and the small, often unnoticed ways we help those around us. Whether it is lending a listening ear, offering a word of encouragement, or giving our time and energy to community projects, each act of service is a thread in the larger tapestry of our collective existence.

Moreover, this book addresses the challenges and ethical considerations that come with a life of service. It confronts the complexities of aid, the delicate balance between helping and enabling, and the critical need for respecting and understanding the cultures and contexts within which we serve. These discussions are crucial, for they remind us that service is not a one-size-fits-all endeavor but a deeply personal and context-sensitive journey that requires wisdom, humility, and continuous learning.

Technology's role in transforming service is also a significant focus here. In our increasingly connected world, new tools have emerged that can enhance our ability to serve—bridging distances, fostering communication, and facilitating the efficient mobilization of resources. Yet, with these advancements come new challenges and responsibilities. We explore how to leverage these tools ethically and effectively, ensuring that technology enhances rather than detracts from the human element of service.

The recognition of service and its celebration also holds a special place in this discourse. Acknowledging and celebrating acts of service not only honors those who give but also inspires others to follow suit. It creates a culture of service that can sustain and expand the impact of individual efforts, weaving them into the larger social fabric. In this light, we discuss how to build and sustain this culture, recognizing the contributions of all who give, regardless of the scale or visibility of their efforts.

As we look to the future, the spirit of service needs nurturing to thrive. This book proposes ways to cultivate and sustain this spirit, ensuring that the legacy of service continues through generations. It calls for a collective commitment to foster an environment where service is valued and supported at every level of society—from individual actions to institutional policies and national initiatives.

In presenting these themes, this book does not merely aim to inform but to inspire. It invites readers to reflect on their own capacity for service and to consider how they might weave their own threads into the ever-expanding tapestry of selfless giving. It is a call to action, urging each of us to consider how we might live a life that not only serves others but also transforms our own—creating a legacy of kindness, compassion, and connectedness that transcends our individual lives.

Thus, this book is an ode to the power of service. It celebrates the extraordinary impact of ordinary acts of giving and the profound joy that can be found in living for others. It is a guide, a reflection, and, most importantly, an invitation to weave your own unique patterns into the grand tapestry of service that enriches our world.

# ONE

# UNDERSTANDING KARMA: THE BASICS OF CAUSE AND EFFECT

Karma is a concept that originates from ancient Indian philosophy and has permeated various cultures and spiritual traditions worldwide. It holds that every action has a consequence, and these consequences unfold, either in this life or in a reincarnated future. This belief system encourages individuals to act with mindfulness and morality, as the effects of their actions will return to them in kind.

At its core, the principle of karma is about the connectivity of actions and outcomes. Each choice made and each action taken sets off a chain of events leading to future consequences. These can be immediate or long-term, affecting the individual directly or rippling out to influence others and the environment. Understanding this interconnection encourages a thoughtful approach to life, where mindfulness in one's actions becomes paramount.

The notion of karma isn't just about the repercussions of one's actions but also about the intention behind those actions. The purity of intention plays a significant role in determining the karma generated. Actions performed with good intentions, even if they inadvertently lead to negative outcomes, are often seen to generate good karma. Conversely, actions taken with harmful intentions are believed to bring about negative karma, regardless of the immediate effects.

This understanding of karma brings with it a responsibility towards ethical living. If one believes that all actions have potential consequences, then there is a greater incentive to act in ways that are not only beneficial to oneself but also to others. This is where the concept seamlessly intersects with the idea of selfless service. By engaging in acts of kindness and service without the expectation of personal gain, individuals contribute positively to the world while creating good karma that benefits all.

Selfless service, when viewed through the lens of karma, becomes a powerful tool for personal and communal transformation. Acts of generosity and kindness don't just aid those on the receiving end; they also contribute to the spiritual and moral growth of the giver. The practice of selfless service cultivates virtues such as empathy, compassion, and humility. It challenges one to look beyond personal desires and to consider the well-being of others, fostering a sense of connectedness with the broader community and the world.

Moreover, karma emphasizes the cumulative effect of actions. Regular engagement in selfless activities gradually transforms one's character, making altruism and service natural extensions of one's being. Over time, these actions become less about deliberate effort and more about instinctual behavior, woven into the very fabric of one's personality.

In practical terms, understanding and applying the concept of karma in daily life can lead to a more conscientious living. It encourages individuals to pause and consider the broader consequences of their actions. This reflection can lead to more deliberate and thoughtful decisions, reducing impulsive behavior that might lead to adverse outcomes. For instance, considering the environmental impact of one's consumption choices or the social implications of one's words and actions can foster a more sustainable and harmonious existence.

Selfless service, inspired by a thorough understanding of karma, acts as a bridge between individual action and collective welfare. It shows that personal growth and societal improvement are not mutually exclusive but are interdependent realities. By embracing the principles of karma, individuals are motivated to act with consideration for the wider impact of their actions, thus contributing to a cycle of positivity and mutual respect among all beings.

In essence, karma is not just a spiritual or philosophical concept but a practical guide for living. It teaches that the quality of one's life is directly related to the quality of one's actions. By choosing actions that are harmonious with the world around us, we weave a life of meaningful interactions and relationships. This life, rich in selfless service, not only elevates one's own experience but also uplifts those around, creating a tapestry of lives interconnected by acts of kindness and understanding. Through this understanding, the true essence of karma is revealed—not as a punitive system, but as a transformative one, encouraging actions that support personal and communal well-being, paving the way for a more thoughtful and compassionate world.

*"True service is a journey, not a destination; it enriches those who give just as much as those who receive, teaching us that in giving, we find ourselves."*

♡♡♡

# TWO

# THE JOY OF GIVING: WHY SELFLESS SERVICE MATTERS

The act of giving is often perceived as a simple transfer of something from one person to another, but its implications and impacts stretch far beyond the immediate moment of exchange. Selfless service, or the act of giving without expecting anything in return, enriches lives and communities in profound ways. It fosters a sense of connection and shared humanity, reminding us that we are not isolated beings but part of a larger, interconnected community.

Selfless service is grounded in the idea that true joy and fulfillment come not from what we receive, but from what we give. This concept challenges the often prevalent societal focus on accumulation and personal gain, suggesting that the path to a truly satisfying life is found in contributing to the well-being of others.

Such service can take many forms, ranging from simple acts like volunteering at a local shelter to more significant commitments like working in public service or contributing to large-scale humanitarian efforts. Regardless of the scale, the underlying principle remains the same: giving selflessly enhances our lives and the lives of others.

One of the most compelling reasons why selfless service matters is its impact on our psychological health. Studies have shown that engaging in acts of kindness can boost mood and decrease stress. This is often referred to as the "helper's high," a state of elevated mood resulting from altruism. More than just a temporary boost, regular engagement in selfless acts has been linked to longer-term improvements in overall mental health. It reduces symptoms of depression and anxiety and increases feelings of social connectedness.

Furthermore, selfless service plays a crucial role in building and strengthening communities. When individuals contribute to their communities without expecting returns, they lay the foundation for a culture of generosity and mutual support.

This can be especially impactful in times of crisis, where communal support structures become lifelines for those affected. By fostering an environment where people are motivated to help each other, communities become more resilient to challenges they might face.

Moreover, selfless giving has a unique way of bridging divides—be they social, economic, or cultural. In a world often marked by division, acts of kindness can be a universal language of compassion. Helping others can break down barriers, fostering understanding and empathy among diverse groups of people. This not only helps in alleviating immediate hardships but also promotes long-term social cohesion and peace.

The impact of selfless service also extends to the moral and ethical development of individuals. Engaging in acts of kindness helps to cultivate virtues such as empathy, compassion, and humility. These qualities are essential for the moral grounding of individuals; they guide us to act ethically and with consideration for the well-being of others. The practice of selfless service offers a pathway to developing these traits, reinforcing the moral fabric of society.

From a broader perspective, selfless service is crucial for addressing many of the systemic issues that plague societies. Whether it's fighting poverty, improving education, or addressing health disparities, these challenges require concerted efforts that prioritize the common good over individual gain. By promoting a culture of giving, societies can mobilize resources and human energy towards creating more equitable and sustainable solutions.

Moreover, engaging in selfless service provides individuals with a sense of purpose and belonging. Many find that in giving, they connect with a larger purpose that transcends their individual lives, aligning them with values such as justice, equity, and compassion. This alignment not only enriches their own lives but also makes them agents of positive change in the world.

Additionally, selfless service teaches gratitude. By helping those in less fortunate circumstances, individuals gain perspective on their own lives, often leading to greater appreciation for what they have. This gratitude can transform their approach to life, encouraging a focus on what truly matters—relationships, community, and helping one another.

Lastly, the joy of giving has a cumulative effect. Each act of kindness can inspire others to act, creating a ripple effect that can spread far beyond the original act. This exponential potential is why selfless service is so powerful—it not only changes the lives of individuals but can transform entire communities and, ultimately, societies.

In essence, selfless service is much more than an act of giving. It is a philosophy of living that enriches the giver and receiver alike, creating a more compassionate and connected world. The joy of giving underscores the profound truth that our greatest joys and our most fulfilling lives are found not in what we acquire, but in what we contribute to the lives of others.

In embracing selfless service, we find that the path to true happiness is through making others happy, weaving a fabric of community bound together by acts of kindness and generosity.

*"Every act of kindness is a thread in the tapestry of humanity; with each thread, we strengthen the whole, weaving a richer narrative of community and compassion."*

♡♡♡

# THREE

# Small Acts, Big Impacts: Stories of Everyday Heroes

Every day, across the globe, ordinary individuals engage in small acts of kindness that yield extraordinary impacts on the lives of others. These everyday heroes are not distinguished by their capes or superpowers but by their compassion, resilience, and willingness to help. Their stories may not always make headlines, but they weave a rich tapestry of generosity and community spirit that holds societies together.

Small acts of service, though they might seem inconsequential in isolation, can collectively transform entire communities. A simple gesture, like helping a neighbor in need or volunteering a few hours at a local charity, can set off a chain of goodwill that reverberates far beyond the initial act.

This cumulative effect underscores the profound influence of seemingly minor deeds, which often ignite a spirit of community engagement and mutual help.

Consider the story of an elderly man who starts his day early to clean up his neighborhood park. Equipped with just a bag and a picker, he meticulously removes litter that accumulates overnight. While his contribution might seem modest, it plays a crucial role in maintaining the beauty and health of a shared community space.

This act not only preserves the environment but also instills a sense of pride and ownership among the local residents, encouraging more people to take active roles in their community's upkeep.

Then, there is the tale of a young woman who tutors children from underprivileged backgrounds. By dedicating a few hours each week, she provides these children with the educational support they lack at home.

Her commitment helps bridge educational gaps, offering her students a better chance at success in school and beyond. This not only enhances their immediate learning but also boosts their confidence and aspirations for the future.

Stories of everyday heroes also include those of individuals who perform acts of kindness that restore faith in humanity during times of crisis. For instance, during natural disasters, ordinary people often emerge as first responders before official help arrives.

They rescue stranded victims, provide first aid, and distribute food and water. Their swift and selfless actions save lives and offer comfort in the face of adversity.

Moreover, consider the impact of someone who simply takes the time to listen. In a world where many people struggle with loneliness and depression, the act of listening can be a profound service. A person who offers a sympathetic ear and a shoulder to lean on can make a significant difference in someone's mental and emotional health. This support can be the turning point for individuals battling mental health issues, giving them strength and hope.

Another impactful small act is that of kindness extended to strangers. Whether it's paying for someone's meal in a line, leaving a generous tip, or helping someone carry heavy bags, these acts of kindness can brighten someone's day and remind them of the goodness in the world. Such gestures often encourage recipients to pay it forward, creating a ripple effect of kindness that spreads through the community.

Furthermore, small acts of environmental conservation, like planting trees or cleaning up beaches, contribute significantly to the health of the planet. Each tree planted helps absorb carbon dioxide, and every piece of trash removed from beaches protects marine life. These actions, though small, play a part in combating global environmental issues like climate change and pollution.

The story of everyday heroes is also about those who advocate for change. Individuals who use their voices to speak out against injustices or work to raise awareness about important issues play a crucial role in societal reform. By initiating conversations and challenging the status quo, they inspire others to join their causes and fight for a better world.

These stories illustrate that the power of small acts should not be underestimated. Each act contributes to a larger narrative of hope, resilience, and community spirit.

Everyday heroes exemplify the best of humanity, showing that each person has the capacity to make a difference. Their actions remind us that heroism is not about extraordinary deeds but about making a positive impact in whatever ways we can.

In essence, the stories of everyday heroes teach us that we all hold the potential to influence the world positively, one small act at a time. They challenge us to look beyond ourselves and consider how our actions, no matter how small, can contribute to a larger good.

By recognizing and celebrating these acts, we not only honor those who perform them but also inspire more people to take up the mantle of service. In doing so, we collectively contribute to a kinder, more compassionate world where small acts lead to big impacts.

*"Service is the art of seeing the need beyond the ask, of listening deeply not just to the words spoken but to the silent pleas of those seeking help."*

# FOUR

# Cultivating Compassion: Building Empathy in Our Lives

Cultivating compassion and building empathy in our lives are essential practices that enhance interpersonal relationships and improve community well-being. Compassion, the emotional response of caring for and wanting to help those who are suffering, along with empathy, the ability to understand and share the feelings of another, are cornerstones of human social interaction that foster a sense of connection and shared humanity.

The development of these qualities is not merely beneficial for creating harmonious relationships but is also crucial for personal mental and emotional well-being. Empathy allows us to perceive the world from another's perspective, enhancing our understanding of the complexities of human emotions and behaviors. Compassion motivates us to take action to alleviate others‘ suffering, enriching our own lives through the fulfillment that comes from helping others.

Understanding the nature of empathy is the first step in cultivating it. Empathy involves more than simply sympathizing with someone; it is about truly engaging with the emotional experiences of others. This can be challenging, as it requires openness and vulnerability, qualities that are sometimes suppressed in competitive, individualistic societies. However, by nurturing these qualities, individuals can develop stronger, more empathetic relationships.

One effective method for enhancing empathy is active listening. This involves paying full attention to the speaker, acknowledging their feelings without judgment, and responding in a way that confirms the emotions have been understood. This practice not only helps in understanding people better but also makes them feel valued and heard, which is a fundamental aspect of empathetic interaction.

Another way to foster empathy is through exposure to diverse life experiences and perspectives. This can be achieved by reading literature, watching films, or engaging in conversations that explore different cultural, social, and personal backgrounds. Such experiences can broaden one's understanding of the human condition, making it easier to relate to others' feelings and experiences.

Practicing mindfulness is also a powerful tool for developing empathy. Mindfulness involves maintaining a moment-by-moment awareness of our thoughts, feelings, bodily sensations, and surrounding environment. This practice helps in managing one's reactions to the emotions and actions of others, allowing for more measured, empathetic responses.

Compassion can be cultivated through acts of kindness and volunteer work. Engaging regularly in community service or simply extending small gestures of kindness in everyday life can reinforce compassionate behaviors. These actions not only benefit recipients but also enhance the giver's emotional well-being, creating a positive feedback loop that strengthens community bonds.

Moreover, teaching compassion and empathy from a young age is crucial. Educational systems that incorporate social and emotional learning programs can play a significant role in this regard. These programs teach children to recognize and manage their emotions, understand others' feelings, and develop caring and constructive relationships. By instilling these values early in life, societies can nurture more empathetic and compassionate future generations.

Reflective practices such as journaling or group discussions about personal experiences with empathy can also deepen one's understanding and ability to express compassion. These reflections can provide insights into personal emotional responses and highlight areas for growth in empathetic understanding.

The benefits of cultivating compassion and building empathy extend beyond personal satisfaction and improved relationships. On a broader scale, these qualities can lead to more cooperative and peaceful societies. When people understand and care for each other, conflicts are more likely to be resolved peacefully, and social injustices are more readily addressed.

However, it's important to manage the emotional toll that empathy and compassion can take. Known as "compassion fatigue," the stress of constantly feeling for others can be mitigated by maintaining a balance between caring for others and self-care. Ensuring that one's own emotional and physical needs are met is essential for sustaining the ability to help others effectively.

In sum, cultivating compassion and building empathy are dynamic processes that require intentionality and practice. By committing to these practices, individuals can enrich their lives and the lives of others, contributing to a more understanding and caring world. This commitment to empathy and compassion not only enhances individual lives but also strengthens the fabric of communities, creating a collective resilience and a shared sense of humanity that can confront the challenges of the future with collective strength and wisdom.

*"In the echoes of gratitude, we find the true reward of service—the realization that our actions have left imprints on hearts and lives beyond our own."*

♡♡♡

# FIVE

# The Ripple Effect: How Kindness Spreads

The concept of the ripple effect, particularly in the context of kindness, is a powerful metaphor for how individual actions can create waves of impact that extend far beyond the initial splash. This phenomenon describes how a single act of kindness can influence others to pass on goodwill, thereby amplifying the initial gesture into a much larger movement of benevolence and compassion. The ripple effect not only illustrates the interconnectedness of human actions but also underscores the significant role that even the smallest deeds can play in shaping the social fabric.

Understanding the ripple effect begins with the acknowledgment that human emotions and behaviors are highly contagious. When someone witnesses an act of kindness, they are not only more likely to feel uplifted but also motivated to replicate this behavior. This cycle of kindness, once initiated, can propagate through a community, increasing the likelihood of more altruistic acts being performed. The beauty of this process lies in its exponential nature;

each act of kindness has the potential to multiply and spread across many individuals and situations.

The initial act that triggers this ripple can be as simple as a smile, a compliment, or a small gesture of assistance. For instance, when a person helps an elderly individual carry groceries to their car, this act of kindness doesn't just end with the help provided. The elderly person feels appreciated and cared for, which improves their mood and might encourage them to extend kindness to someone else. Similarly, onlookers who witness this small deed are reminded of the value of compassion and are often inspired to perform their own acts of kindness. Thus, the original act creates a cascade of positive interactions.

The ripple effect of kindness is further reinforced through the emotional state it engenders. Psychological studies have shown that performing or observing acts of kindness releases serotonin, a neurotransmitter responsible for feelings of satisfaction and well-being. This not only enhances the mood of the giver and receiver but also of those who observe the act. It's a chain reaction that promotes an overall sense of community and well-being, making kindness a compelling force for communal harmony.

Moreover, the spread of kindness through the ripple effect can significantly impact societal norms and values. When acts of kindness become more frequent within a community, they contribute to a culture of generosity and compassion. This cultural shift can transform the way people interact on a daily basis, promoting more empathetic and supportive communities. In schools, for example, programs that encourage acts of kindness have been shown to reduce bullying and enhance students' sense of cooperation and trust.

The ripple effect also holds a profound implication for leadership and organizational behavior. In corporate settings, when leaders demonstrate kindness and concern for the well-being of their employees, it sets a tone for the entire organization. Employees feel valued and respected, which enhances their job satisfaction and productivity. They are also more likely to mirror these behaviors in their interactions with colleagues and clients, enhancing the organization's overall environment and even its brand image.

Importantly, the ripple effect of kindness transcends cultural and national boundaries. Acts of kindness can bridge gaps between diverse groups, fostering mutual respect and understanding. During humanitarian crises or natural disasters, the outpouring of support and aid from around the world is a powerful demonstration of how kindness can unite disparate groups towards a common goal of alleviating suffering.

However, sustaining the ripple effect of kindness requires conscious effort and commitment. It involves cultivating personal virtues and continually choosing to act kindly, even in challenging situations. Additionally, it requires the recognition and celebration of acts of kindness, no matter how small, to reinforce the value of these actions within society.

The potential of the ripple effect to transform society is immense. By adopting a mindset that recognizes the impact of our actions on others, we can contribute to a global culture of kindness. This culture not only improves individual lives but also has the potential to address larger societal issues by fostering an environment where cooperative and altruistic behaviors are the norm.

In essence, the ripple effect of kindness is a testament to the power of human agency. Each person has the capability to initiate waves of positive change through simple, thoughtful actions. By embracing the potential of these acts to inspire others, we can collectively contribute to a more compassionate and harmonious world. This understanding encourages us to act intentionally, with the knowledge that our smallest deeds can lead to significant, widespread change, weaving a tapestry of kindness that can envelop communities and eventually, the globe.

*"Empathy is the bridge between diversity and unity; through service, we cross this bridge repeatedly, discovering the universal truths shared across all divides."*

♡♡♡

# SIX

# VOLUNTEERING: A PATH TO PERSONAL GROWTH

Volunteering is often heralded as a noble endeavor, a selfless act aimed at improving the lives of others. However, beyond its altruistic appeal, volunteering serves as a powerful vehicle for personal growth. It provides individuals with the opportunity to learn new skills, expand their social networks, enhance their sense of well-being, and deepen their understanding of the world around them. This multifaceted impact makes volunteering not just a way to help others but also a significant avenue for self-improvement and personal development.

At the heart of volunteering lies the concept of giving one's time and energy without the expectation of monetary reward. This aspect of selflessness in volunteering is crucial, as it shifts the focus from personal gain to community service. Yet, the paradox of volunteering is that while it aims at benefiting others, it invariably enriches the volunteer's own life. This enrichment comes through various forms—emotional, social, intellectual, and even physical.

Emotionally, volunteering has been shown to boost personal happiness and satisfaction. Engaging in community service activities can enhance one's mood and provide a sense of purpose and fulfillment. Studies have repeatedly found that those who volunteer experience lower rates of depression, increased life satisfaction, and improved overall mental health. The act of helping others triggers the release of endorphins, the brain's natural mood elevators, which can create what is known as the "helper's high." This emotional lift is not just temporary; regular volunteers report sustained levels of happiness and increased self-esteem.

Socially, volunteering opens up new avenues for networking. It allows individuals to meet people from diverse backgrounds and form connections based on shared values and common goals. These networks can be invaluable, providing both personal and professional support. Through volunteering, individuals can enhance their social skills, learn to work as part of a team, and develop leadership abilities. For many, these social interactions are pivotal, offering a sense of community and belonging that might be absent in other areas of their lives.

Intellectually, volunteering offers opportunities to learn new skills or deepen existing ones. Whether it's organizing events, managing projects, or providing direct services, volunteers often encounter challenges that require creative problem-solving. This hands-on experience can be particularly beneficial for career development, as it allows individuals to apply theoretical knowledge in practical settings. Furthermore, volunteering can expose individuals to new interests and passions, guiding career choices and academic pursuits.

Physically, certain types of volunteering activities can improve one's physical health. Activities that involve physical labor, such as building homes for the needy, cleaning up parks, or participating in charity runs, promote physical fitness. Moreover, the positive emotional effects of volunteering, such as reduced stress and anxiety, can lead to better physical health outcomes, including lower blood pressure and a longer lifespan.

Moreover, volunteering also serves as a powerful tool for cultural and global understanding. For those who volunteer internationally or in culturally diverse environments, the experience can be a profound exercise in cultural exchange and empathy development. Volunteers often find themselves immersed in communities with different customs and languages, pushing them to develop a deeper understanding of and respect for other ways of life. This cultural sensitivity is an invaluable skill in today's globalized world.

Volunteering also fosters resilience. Regular engagement in community service can help individuals develop a stronger sense of resilience by exposing them to real-world challenges and providing them with opportunities to navigate difficult situations. The problem-solving and emotional coping skills gained through volunteering are transferable to personal and professional challenges, making individuals better equipped to handle adversity.

In a broader sense, volunteering contributes to a greater societal awareness. Volunteers are often at the frontline of social issues, such as homelessness, poverty, and inequality. This direct exposure increases their awareness of the complexities and depths of these issues and can ignite a lifelong commitment to advocacy and social change.

Finally, volunteering is an act of citizenship. It is a way for individuals to give back to their communities, make a tangible impact, and participate actively in the democratic process. In this way, volunteering nurtures a sense of civic responsibility and strengthens the fabric of society.

The path of volunteering offers a rich landscape for personal growth. It challenges individuals to step out of their comfort zones, encourages them to forge meaningful connections, and instills a deep sense of satisfaction and purpose. By engaging in volunteer work, individuals not only contribute to the well-being of others but also embark on a profound journey of self-discovery and development. The transformative power of volunteering thus lies not only in the help that is given but also in the growth that is gained, making it a truly reciprocal exchange.

*"The spirit of service is nurtured by persistence and resilience; it is the commitment to continue giving, even when faced with challenges and uncertainties."*

♡♡♡

# SEVEN

# Mindfulness in Service: Being Present While Helping Others

Mindfulness in service refers to the practice of being fully present and engaged in the moment while performing acts of service for others. It involves a conscious focus on the here and now, paying attention to one's thoughts, feelings, and actions as well as the needs and responses of others. This approach not only enhances the quality of the service provided but also deepens the personal satisfaction and effectiveness of the volunteer or caregiver. Integrating mindfulness into service activities can transform routine interactions into meaningful experiences, promoting both personal growth and profound social impact.

The practice of mindfulness originates from ancient meditation practices but has been adapted in modern times to a variety of contexts, including education, psychotherapy, and even business. In the context of service, mindfulness involves a deliberate attentiveness to the act of helping, fostering a deeper connection between the giver and the receiver. This connection is not merely emotional or psychological; it also has practical implications, enhancing the effectiveness of the help provided.

Being mindful while serving others means being aware of one's own mental and emotional state. This self-awareness is crucial because it influences how one interacts with others. For instance, a volunteer who is aware of their own stress or bias may be better able to manage these feelings and prevent them from affecting their interactions. By remaining mentally and emotionally present, volunteers and caregivers can provide more compassionate and tailored assistance, addressing the real needs of those they are helping rather than operating on auto-pilot or making assumptions.

Mindfulness also enhances empathy, the ability to understand and share the feelings of another. By focusing fully on the person they are helping, volunteers can better perceive the subtle nuances of that person's emotions and responses. This empathetic connection is vital in many service settings, such as counseling, healthcare, and social work, where understanding the emotional state of another can be crucial to providing effective support. Empathy, strengthened by mindfulness, allows for more responsive and adaptive interactions, which are essential for meeting complex human needs.

Moreover, mindfulness in service helps to maintain emotional resilience. Engaging in service, particularly in challenging settings like hospitals, disaster zones, or areas of socio-economic deprivation, can be emotionally taxing. Mindfulness practices, such as focused breathing or mindful observation, can help volunteers manage their emotions and prevent burnout. These techniques provide a way to decompress and reflect, ensuring that caregivers maintain their mental health and continue to serve effectively.

The benefits of mindfulness in service extend beyond the individual to impact the broader community. When service workers are mindful, they set a tone of attentiveness and respect within their interactions, which can foster a general atmosphere of care and dignity. This atmosphere can be particularly transformative in environments where individuals are vulnerable or have experienced trauma, as it promotes a sense of safety and trust.

Mindfulness in service also contributes to a culture of ethical behavior and integrity. By being fully present, individuals are more likely to act conscientiously and make decisions that reflect a deep consideration of their impact on others. This ethical sensitivity is crucial in many service roles, where decisions can significantly affect the lives of others. Mindful service ensures that actions are not only effective but also just and compassionate.

Practicing mindfulness while helping others requires training and regular practice. Service organizations can foster this by providing workshops and resources on mindfulness techniques. These might include training in meditation, guided reflection sessions, or the integration of mindfulness exercises into daily routines. Encouraging a culture of mindfulness not only enhances the individual experiences of volunteers but also improves the overall effectiveness and ethical standards of the organizations they represent.

Furthermore, integrating mindfulness into service allows for moments of personal reflection and growth. Volunteers often find that through mindful service, they gain insights into their own lives and challenges. This reflective process can lead to greater self-understanding and personal development, making mindfulness a mutually beneficial practice.

Mindfulness in service is not merely a tool for enhancing the effectiveness of helping others; it is a transformative practice that enriches the interactions between the helper and the helped. It deepens the impact of service work, promotes emotional and ethical development, and strengthens community bonds. By being fully present in acts of service, individuals not only provide better assistance but also engage in a profound process of personal and communal growth, embodying the true spirit of service.

*"Technology in service should enhance, not replace, the human connection; it is a tool to bridge distances but not to distance us from the true essence of helping."*

# EIGHT

# GRATITUDE IN ACTION: APPRECIATING THE WORLD AROUND US

Gratitude in action is a concept that extends the feeling of thankfulness into deliberate expressions that positively impact the world around us. It involves recognizing the abundance in one's life and actively finding ways to give back, thereby creating a cycle of generosity and appreciation. This practice not only enriches the lives of those on the receiving end but also deeply enhances the well-being of the giver, fostering a sense of connectedness and purpose in a world that often emphasizes division and material gain.

The essence of gratitude in action lies in the transformation of an internal feeling into external actions. It goes beyond merely feeling grateful to making a tangible impact through thoughtful deeds. These actions can range from small gestures, like saying thank you or sending a heartfelt note, to larger commitments such as volunteering, donating to charity, or helping someone in need. Each act, regardless of its size, is a step towards a more empathetic and connected society.

Engaging in gratitude can profoundly affect one's mental and emotional health. Psychological research consistently shows that gratitude is strongly correlated with greater happiness. People who practice gratitude regularly report fewer aches and pains, show more resilience against stress, experience fewer feelings of isolation, and enjoy more satisfying relationships. This is because gratitude helps individuals focus on what they have rather than what they lack, which shifts the mindset from scarcity and competition to abundance and cooperation.

Moreover, gratitude in action influences not just individuals but also communities. When people act out of gratitude, they contribute to a positive environment where kindness and generosity flourish. For example, a community project initiated as an expression of thanks to a neighborhood can inspire others to contribute, strengthening community bonds and increasing everyone's sense of belonging and security. These projects often lead to more robust networks of support and collaboration, which are essential for addressing broader societal challenges.

In the workplace, gratitude can transform organizational dynamics. When leaders and employees regularly acknowledge and appreciate each other's efforts, a culture of appreciation is cultivated. This culture can lead to increased job satisfaction, higher morale, and reduced employee turnover. Gratitude in action within corporate environments can also manifest through corporate social responsibility initiatives, where businesses give back to communities as a way to express thanks for their success and support.

Educationally, integrating gratitude into curricula from an early age can have long-lasting effects. Teaching children to express thanks and give back to their community fosters empathy, emotional intelligence, and a strong moral foundation. These skills are crucial for personal development and are highly valued in professional and personal relationships throughout life.

Gratitude also plays a critical role in environmental stewardship. Recognizing the earth's bounty and beauty can inspire actions to protect and preserve it. This might involve activities such as planting trees, cleaning up local parks, or engaging in conservation efforts. By taking action to express gratitude for the natural world, individuals contribute to the sustainability of the planet for future generations.

The practice of gratitude in action also includes overcoming obstacles to generosity, such as envy or a sense of entitlement. By choosing to focus on gratitude, individuals can cultivate a mindset that transcends these barriers and fosters an inclusive approach to life. This mindset encourages looking beyond oneself, understanding one's privilege, and using it to uplift others. This approach not only resolves feelings of discontent but also builds a legacy of kindness.

Moreover, gratitude is deeply reciprocal. Acts of gratitude encourage a cycle of giving that often returns to the giver in various forms—whether as direct reciprocation or through the satisfaction of having made a positive difference. The social bonds strengthened by these exchanges are fundamental to human well-being and societal stability.

In a broader sense, gratitude in action can be seen as a form of social activism. By advocating for and practicing equitable sharing of resources, acknowledging the contributions of others, and supporting social justice initiatives, gratitude can influence systemic change. It challenges the status quo by prioritizing cooperation and appreciation over competition and indifference.

Gratitude in action is a powerful principle for personal and social transformation. It encourages individuals to not only feel grateful but also to act on this gratitude in ways that benefit themselves and the world around them. Through this practice, gratitude becomes more than just a personal virtue; it becomes a communal asset that can lead to a more just, generous, and interconnected world. Thus, by embedding gratitude into daily actions, we can collectively foster an environment where appreciation, generosity, and mutual respect are the norm, ultimately creating a more harmonious and thriving society.

*"Recognition in service is not about seeking applause but about acknowledging the collective efforts that foster change and inspire further acts of kindness."*

# NINE

# Overcoming Barriers to Service: Common Challenges and Solutions

Engaging in acts of service, whether through volunteerism, community work, or professional roles focused on helping others, can be deeply fulfilling and beneficial both for individuals and society. However, potential volunteers and organizations often face significant barriers that can hinder the effectiveness and reach of their efforts. Addressing these challenges requires a nuanced understanding of their causes and the implementation of strategic solutions that can facilitate more accessible and impactful service opportunities.

One of the primary barriers to engaging in service is the lack of time. Many individuals feel that their daily responsibilities—whether job, family, or education—leave little room for volunteer activities. This can be particularly true in societies where long work hours are the norm and where economic pressures necessitate multiple jobs or extended workdays. To overcome this barrier, organizations can offer more flexible volunteering options that accommodate different schedules and commitments. This could include short-term projects, remote volunteering opportunities, or roles that require varying levels of time commitment throughout the year. Additionally, promoting the concept of micro-volunteering, where tasks are broken down into small, manageable actions that can be completed quickly, can also help integrate service into busy lives.

Another significant barrier is the lack of skills or experience. Potential volunteers often feel that they do not possess the necessary skills to contribute effectively or fear that their lack of experience might be more of a burden than a help. To address this, organizations can provide training and support for volunteers. This not only helps volunteers feel more prepared and valued but also enhances the quality of service provided. On the other hand, it's essential for organizations to clearly communicate the variety of roles available, highlighting that there are numerous ways to contribute that do not require specialized skills and that every effort, no matter how small, is valuable.

Financial constraints also pose a considerable challenge to service engagement. Many would-be volunteers are deterred by the costs associated with volunteering, such as travel expenses, materials, or even the opportunity cost of unpaid leave from work. To mitigate these issues, organizations can seek funding to cover such expenses for volunteers or provide stipends to make volunteering more economically viable. Additionally, creating partnerships with businesses that encourage employee volunteerism through sponsored programs can also alleviate financial pressures on individual volunteers.

Geographical barriers can also limit service opportunities, especially in rural or underserved areas where there may be fewer organizations and resources available. Expanding outreach efforts into these areas or utilizing digital platforms to facilitate virtual volunteering can help bridge the geographical divide. For instance, online tutoring, digital marketing for nonprofits, or remote administrative support are all valuable services that can be provided regardless of physical location.

Cultural barriers and lack of diversity within organizations can also discourage participation. When potential volunteers do not see themselves represented in an organization, they may feel unwelcome or unsure if their contributions will be valued. Organizations must strive for inclusivity by actively seeking to diversify their volunteer base and leadership. This can be achieved through targeted outreach, collaboration with community leaders from diverse backgrounds, and sensitivity training for staff and volunteers to create a more welcoming environment for everyone.

Furthermore, bureaucratic hurdles such as complicated application processes, background checks, and training requirements can deter potential volunteers. While these procedures are often necessary for safety and organizational integrity, simplifying these processes and making them as transparent as possible can encourage more people to engage in service. Providing clear instructions, support during the application process, and timely feedback can help mitigate the intimidation or frustration associated with bureaucratic red tape.

Lastly, burnout and lack of recognition can demotivate volunteers. Continuous engagement in service, especially in emotionally demanding roles, can lead to exhaustion unless proper support systems are in place. Organizations should implement strategies to prevent burnout by offering regular training, support groups, and adequate breaks. Recognizing and celebrating the contributions of volunteers through awards, thank-you events, and public acknowledgment can also enhance motivation and the feeling of being valued.

Overcoming these barriers requires a concerted effort by organizations, communities, and governments to create an environment that facilitates and encourages service. By addressing these challenges with thoughtful solutions, service opportunities can become more accessible, enjoyable, and effective, allowing a broader range of individuals to contribute to the betterment of society. Through such efforts, the spirit of service can be sustained and expanded, leading to a more compassionate and proactive community.

*"Every community has its own rhythm of need and response; effective service listens to this rhythm, finding the pace and patterns that resonate deeply within."*

ᑭᑭᑭ

# TEN

# Building a Community of Care: Working Together for a Better World

Building a community of care involves nurturing a culture where individuals collectively commit to supporting each other's well-being and working towards a common good. This concept transcends the traditional notion of community as merely a group of people living in proximity to one another. Instead, it envisions a dynamic network of relationships driven by shared values of empathy, responsibility, and mutual aid. In a community of care, members actively participate in creating a supportive environment that enhances the quality of life for all its members, fostering a sense of belonging and purpose that is crucial for societal progress.

The foundation of such a community lies in recognizing the interconnectedness of all members and the belief that the well-being of each individual is intrinsically linked to the well-being of the community as a whole. This understanding prompts members to look beyond their personal interests and consider the broader implications of their actions. It cultivates a mindset where people feel responsible not only for themselves but also for their neighbors, leading to more thoughtful and compassionate interactions.

One of the key strategies for building a community of care is fostering open and ongoing communication. Regular dialogue helps to bridge gaps between different community members, allowing for a better understanding of diverse perspectives and needs. This can be facilitated through community meetings, social gatherings, and digital platforms that encourage interaction and discussion. Effective communication also involves active listening skills, where members genuinely pay attention to each other's concerns and suggestions, creating an atmosphere of trust and respect.

Another critical element is inclusivity. A community of care must strive to be inclusive, ensuring that all members, regardless of age, race, gender, socioeconomic status, or physical ability, have the opportunity to participate fully in community life. This involves not only open invitation but also proactive measures to remove barriers that might prevent participation. For instance, providing language translation services, ensuring accessibility for people with disabilities, and creating safe spaces for marginalized groups are all actions that contribute to an inclusive community.

Collaboration and partnership within the community are also vital. Many societal challenges are complex and cannot be addressed by individuals or single entities alone. Collaborative efforts that bring together various stakeholders—residents, local businesses, nonprofits, and government agencies—can leverage diverse resources and expertise to tackle issues more effectively. Partnerships can be formal or informal, but they should be grounded in mutual goals and shared benefits.

Empowering community members to take leadership roles is another essential aspect of building a community of care. Empowerment involves providing the skills, resources, and opportunities necessary for individuals to effectively contribute to community development. This can include leadership training programs, grants for community projects, and mentorship opportunities. Empowered individuals are more likely to initiate positive changes and inspire others to get involved, creating a proactive community culture.

Education and awareness-raising are also crucial in cultivating a caring community. By educating members about issues such as mental health, environmental sustainability, and social justice, communities can develop a deeper understanding of the challenges they face and the roles they can play in addressing them. Awareness campaigns can be facilitated through workshops, seminars, and community-based learning projects that engage members actively and provide practical knowledge and skills.

Moreover, recognizing and celebrating the contributions of community members is important for sustaining motivation and acknowledging the value of care work. Celebrations and public acknowledgments of individuals and groups who contribute significantly to the community can reinforce positive behaviors and encourage others to contribute as well.

Additionally, providing support systems within the community is essential. These systems can include health services, emotional counseling, financial aid, and other forms of support that ensure all members can access the help they need when they need it. Effective support systems not only assist individuals in overcoming personal challenges but also strengthen the community by preventing crises and reducing long-term problems.

Finally, building a community of care requires a commitment to continuous improvement. This involves regular assessment of community needs, feedback mechanisms to evaluate the effectiveness of community initiatives, and a willingness to adapt and evolve strategies over time. Continuous improvement helps ensure that the community remains responsive to its members' changing needs and is resilient in the face of new challenges.

In essence, building a community of care is about creating a sustainable framework where everyone is valued and supported. It requires thoughtful planning, active participation, and ongoing dedication to nurturing an environment where everyone can thrive. By working together for a better world, communities can become stronger, more cohesive, and better equipped to face the challenges of the future, embodying the very essence of what it means to care for one another.

*"Leadership in service is about humility and vision; it's about leading by example and inspiring others to join in the relentless pursuit of bettering our world."*

ჸჸჸ

# ELEVEN

# Sustainable Service: Ensuring Our Efforts Last

Sustainable service is a critical concept that ensures the longevity and effectiveness of volunteer efforts and community programs. It focuses on creating initiatives that are not only impactful in the short term but also durable and adaptable over time, supporting long-lasting benefits for the community and the environment. The key to sustainable service lies in thoughtful planning, resource management, and community involvement, ensuring that the projects and efforts initiated today continue to thrive and adapt in the future.

The first step towards sustainable service is the thorough assessment of community needs. This involves engaging with the community to understand its unique challenges and resources. By involving community members in the needs assessment, organizations can ensure that the services provided are relevant and address the actual needs of the community rather than imposed solutions that may not align with local priorities. This bottom-up approach helps in building programs that are more likely to be accepted and sustained by the community.

Another important aspect of sustainable service is designing projects with a long-term perspective. This means considering not just the immediate outcomes but also how the projects will continue to operate in the future. Sustainability in this context involves careful resource management, including planning for financial sustainability, training local leaders, and developing mechanisms for ongoing support and maintenance. For example, a health initiative should include not only treatment components but also education, prevention, and partnerships with local healthcare providers to ensure continuity.

Financial sustainability is crucial and can be one of the most challenging aspects to secure. Sustainable service projects often require initial funding, but they should also have a plan for generating income or securing ongoing funding sources. This could be through local government support, private donations, or income-generating activities related to the service provided. Establishing a diversified funding base helps protect programs from economic shifts and funding cuts.

Capacity building within the community is also essential for sustainability. This involves training and empowering local individuals to lead and manage community projects. By developing local leadership, organizations ensure that the community possesses the skills and knowledge necessary to continue the projects regardless of external support. This empowerment also fosters a sense of ownership and responsibility among community members, which is critical for the long-term success and sustainability of service efforts.

Technological sustainability should also be considered, especially in projects that rely on technology to function. This involves choosing technology that is appropriate for the local context and sustainable in terms of maintenance and operation. For example, using renewable energy sources like solar power in remote areas can be more sustainable than relying on diesel generators, which require continual fuel supply and maintenance.

Environmental sustainability is another key component, ensuring that service projects do not harm but rather help the environment. This can be integrated into every project by considering the environmental impact and opting for eco-friendly materials and practices. For instance, a construction project for community housing should use sustainable materials and techniques that minimize environmental impact while enhancing the community's resilience to environmental changes.

Monitoring and evaluation are critical for sustainable service. Regular assessment of projects not only measures their impact but also identifies areas for improvement. This ongoing evaluation ensures that the services remain relevant and effective over time and adapt to changing conditions or needs. Effective monitoring and evaluation systems also build credibility and transparency, attracting more support from funders and community members.

Finally, fostering partnerships is essential in sustainable service. Collaborations with local governments, other non-profits, businesses, and international organizations can provide additional resources and support, enhancing the scope and impact of service projects. These partnerships can also offer new insights and approaches, improving the overall strategy for sustainability.

Sustainable service requires a comprehensive approach that encompasses careful planning, community involvement, resource management, and ongoing evaluation. By focusing on these elements, service initiatives can transcend being temporary fixes and transform into enduring sources of support that empower communities and foster a healthier, more sustainable environment.

The goal of sustainable service is to create a legacy of positive change that continues to benefit future generations, establishing a foundation of continuous improvement and lasting impact.

***"Sustainability in service is creating initiatives that outlast our involvement; it's planting seeds of change that grow roots deep in the community long after we've gone."***

♡♡♡

# TWELVE

# The Power of Listening: Understanding Needs in Service

The power of listening is a fundamental component in the field of service, whether it is in healthcare, education, social work, or any other area focused on helping and supporting others. Effective listening goes beyond merely hearing words; it involves understanding, empathy, and responsiveness. When service providers genuinely listen to those they serve, they can better identify and address the underlying issues and needs, creating more impactful and meaningful interactions.

Listening is an active process that requires full engagement and attentiveness. It is about making a conscious effort to understand the perspectives, feelings, and needs of others without immediate judgment or interruption. This kind of deep listening builds trust between the service provider and the recipient, which is crucial for effective service delivery. When individuals feel heard and understood, they are more likely to open up and share critical information that can aid in their support and care.

In the context of social services, for example, practitioners who excel at listening are able to discern not only the explicit needs of their clients but also the implicit, unspoken concerns that may be just as crucial. This could include signs of mental health struggles, familial pressures, or hidden crises that are not immediately apparent. By tuning into these subtleties, service providers can tailor their interventions more accurately and effectively, providing not just generic solutions but personalized support that addresses the specific circumstances of each individual.

The power of listening also plays a significant role in conflict resolution. In situations where tensions and disagreements arise, the act of listening can help de-escalate conflicts by showing respect for different viewpoints. This does not necessarily mean agreeing with the other person's perspective but acknowledging their right to have one. Such recognition can pave the way for more constructive dialogues, where solutions are sought after understanding all sides rather than imposing one's own views.

Moreover, listening is essential for fostering inclusivity and diversity within communities and organizations. In a world that is incredibly diverse in cultures, backgrounds, and experiences, the ability to listen and learn from one another is invaluable. It helps to bridge gaps between different social groups, promoting a more inclusive environment where all voices are heard and valued. This inclusivity strengthens community bonds and enhances collaborative efforts, which are key to successful service initiatives.

Effective listening also involves non-verbal cues such as body language, facial expressions, and tone of voice, which can sometimes communicate more than words. Being attuned to these non-verbal signals can provide deeper insights into a person's emotions and reactions, which are important for understanding their true response to a situation. For instance, someone might verbally express agreement with a proposed action plan but their body language could suggest hesitance or doubt. Recognizing these discrepancies allows service providers to address any underlying concerns that might not be explicitly stated.

Training and development in listening skills are thus crucial for individuals involved in service. Workshops, role-playing exercises, and other training programs can enhance listening skills, teaching individuals how to ask open-ended questions, show empathy, and provide feedback that acknowledges and builds on what has been communicated. Such skills are not only valuable professionally but are also beneficial in personal relationships and everyday interactions.

Listening is also an ongoing learning process. Each interaction provides an opportunity to practice and refine this skill. It involves a continuous cycle of listening, learning, and adapting, which can lead to more effective and responsive service over time. Additionally, fostering a culture of listening within organizations can lead to improved teamwork, more innovative ideas, and a more harmonious work environment.

Furthermore, in the age of digital communication, the importance of listening extends to online platforms. Service providers must be adept at interpreting written communications and responding appropriately, which requires a different set of listening (or reading) skills. This includes being sensitive to the tone of online interactions and understanding the context behind written messages, which can often be misinterpreted without the cues available in face-to-face communication.

In conclusion, the power of listening in the context of service is immense. It is not just a passive act but a dynamic process that involves empathy, attentiveness, and responsiveness. By mastering the art of listening, service providers can significantly enhance the quality of care and support they offer, leading to better outcomes and stronger relationships. Ultimately, listening is about respecting the dignity and worth of every individual, acknowledging their experiences, and validating their feelings, which is the cornerstone of any effective service-oriented interaction.

*"Service transcends cultural barriers; it speaks the universal language of compassion, understood by hearts willing to listen, learn, and help."*

# THIRTEEN

# Empowerment through Education: Teaching as a Form of Service

Empowerment through education stands as one of the most profound forms of service, impacting individuals and communities by fostering independence, critical thinking, and socioeconomic mobility. Education as a service extends beyond the traditional classroom setting, encompassing a wide range of learning experiences that enable individuals to grow, participate fully in society, and take control of their lives. This transformative approach not only benefits the direct recipients but also has a ripple effect across generations and communities, making it a cornerstone of sustainable development.

## The Foundations of Educational Empowerment

At its core, empowerment through education is about providing the tools and opportunities for individuals to build knowledge and skills, which in turn enables them to make informed decisions and shape their own destinies. This form of service is rooted in the belief that education should be accessible to all, regardless of one's background, financial status, or geographic location. It involves breaking down barriers to education that many face—be it poverty, discrimination, or cultural restrictions—thus leveling the playing field and providing a ladder out of disadvantage.

## Education as a Tool for Societal Change

Education serves as a powerful tool for societal change by promoting equality and protecting rights. Literate and educated individuals are more likely to participate in the democratic process, access better job opportunities, and demand justice, thereby contributing to the overall health and governance of their communities. Moreover, education in areas such as health, financial literacy, and law empowers individuals to improve their living conditions, manage their resources wisely, and navigate systems that affect their daily lives.

## The Role of Educators in Empowerment

Educators play a pivotal role in this process. Their task transcends the mere transmission of information; they are facilitators of learning who inspire curiosity and encourage critical thinking. Effective educators adapt their teaching methods to meet the diverse needs of their students, creating inclusive environments that respect and incorporate different perspectives and learning styles. They are also mentors and role models who demonstrate values such as empathy, resilience, and integrity.

## Challenges in Educational Empowerment

Despite its potential, the path to empowerment through education is fraught with challenges. Inequities in educational access and quality persist, with disadvantaged groups often receiving substandard resources. Overcoming these challenges requires systemic change—investment in educational infrastructure, teacher training, and curricular reforms that prioritize critical thinking over rote learning.

Moreover, the digital divide has become increasingly prominent, especially highlighted by global shifts towards online learning. Ensuring that all students have access to digital tools and the internet is crucial for modern education. Teachers and institutions must also be adept at incorporating technology into their teaching to enhance learning rather than widen existing gaps.

## Community Involvement in Educational Empowerment

Community involvement is essential in educational empowerment. Local communities can support schools and learning programs by providing resources, volunteering, and creating a culture that values education. Community-led educational initiatives are particularly effective because they are tailored to the specific needs and contexts of the community, making learning relevant and engaging.

## Education Beyond Academics

Empowerment through education also involves going beyond traditional academic subjects to include life skills education—such as emotional intelligence, conflict resolution, and practical financial skills. These competencies are crucial for personal development and success in life outside the classroom. Furthermore, education can be a powerful counter to prevailing social issues like prejudice and inequality by fostering an understanding of diverse cultures and perspectives.

**Lifelong Learning**

Education as a form of service is not limited to childhood or formal education settings; it extends into adult education and lifelong learning. Adults returning to education to enhance their skills or change careers can be profoundly empowered by learning opportunities that allow them to adapt to changing economic landscapes and personal circumstances.

**Global Perspective and Cooperation**

On a global scale, educational empowerment can contribute to international development goals. Cooperation between countries, through educational exchanges and aid programs, can help raise educational standards worldwide. Such international collaboration not only aids in addressing global educational disparities but also enriches the educational experience by exposing educators and students to diverse practices and perspectives.

In essence, empowerment through education as a form of service is a multi-faceted endeavor that involves a commitment from individuals, educators, communities, and governments. It is a dynamic and continuous process that adapts to the evolving needs of society and the global landscape. By valuing and investing in education, we lay the groundwork for a more just, equitable, and enlightened world, demonstrating that teaching, in its most inclusive and comprehensive form, is indeed one of the highest forms of service.

*"Inclusive service means everyone has a role to play, a contribution to make; diversity in helping hands brings richness and resilience to solutions."*

♡♡♡

# FOURTEEN

# HEALING WORDS: THE IMPACT OF ENCOURAGEMENT AND SUPPORT

The power of language in shaping human experience cannot be understated. Words have the capacity to heal, to soothe, to empower, and to affirm. In the realm of service and care, the strategic use of healing words—those that offer encouragement and support—can significantly affect individuals' emotional, psychological, and even physical well-being. Understanding the impact of these healing words and how they can be effectively used in various contexts is vital for anyone engaged in the service of others, whether as educators, healthcare providers, counselors, or social workers.

**The Therapeutic Power of Words**

At its core, the use of healing words is about utilizing language to facilitate positive change in individuals and communities. Words of encouragement do not merely convey information but also emotional content that can help individuals cope with challenges, overcome difficulties, and feel supported and valued. For instance, in clinical settings, how medical professionals communicate diagnoses and treatments can greatly influence how patients perceive their conditions and their outlooks on recovery. Positive language can instill hope and resilience, while negative language might lead to despair and withdrawal.

**Psychological Underpinnings**

The psychological impact of words is rooted in their ability to influence thought patterns. Positive affirmations and supportive language can help individuals reframe negative thoughts and develop a more optimistic perspective. This cognitive restructuring is a fundamental technique used in various therapeutic settings, including cognitive-behavioral therapy (CBT). By encouraging a more positive outlook, healing words can directly impact mental health, reducing symptoms of anxiety and depression, and boosting overall emotional well-being.

**Words as Social Connectors**

Encouragement and support through language also play a crucial role in strengthening social bonds. In times of crisis or distress, words that convey empathy, understanding, and solidarity can be particularly powerful. They affirm the individual's feelings and experiences, validating their emotions and making them feel seen and heard. This validation is crucial for building trust and rapport, which are foundational to effective support networks. Social support, facilitated through communicative affirmations, is linked to better health outcomes, including lower mortality rates and increased resilience against stress.

### Cultural Considerations

The impact of healing words also varies across different cultural contexts. What is considered encouraging or supportive in one culture may not be perceived the same way in another. This cultural variability necessitates a sensitive approach to communication, one that is informed by an understanding of cultural norms, values, and expressions of empathy and support. For service providers working in multicultural environments, cultural competence—being aware of and respectful towards different cultural perspectives—is essential for the effective use of healing words.

### Educational Settings

In educational environments, the use of supportive and encouraging language by teachers and staff can dramatically influence students' self-esteem, motivation, and performance. Positive feedback, when given effectively, helps students develop a growth mindset—the belief that their abilities can improve over time with effort and perseverance. This mindset is crucial for lifelong learning and can significantly alter students' educational trajectories. Conversely, negative language or criticism can diminish students' drive and self-worth, potentially stunting their educational growth.

### Workplace Environments

Similarly, in the workplace, managers and colleagues can use healing words to foster a positive organizational culture. Recognizing employees' efforts, providing constructive feedback, and communicating during times of change with reassuring and supportive language can help maintain morale and increase job satisfaction and productivity. In such environments, healing words help create a sense of security and community, crucial for organizational success.

**Challenges in Using Healing Words**

Despite their benefits, the effective use of healing words is not without challenges. It requires emotional intelligence, the ability to read social cues, and adapt communication styles to the emotional states of others. Additionally, there is the risk of over-dependence, where individuals may rely too heavily on external validation rather than developing their own resilience and self-validation mechanisms.

**Training and Practice**

To overcome these challenges, training in communication skills should be a staple for professionals in all service capacities. Workshops, role-playing exercises, and mentorship programs can help individuals learn how to convey empathy and support effectively. Furthermore, regular reflection and feedback on communication practices can aid service providers in refining their use of language to ensure it consistently heals and uplifts.

Healing words—those that provide encouragement and support—play an indispensable role in fostering well-being and resilience in individuals and communities. Their correct application can transform interactions and relationships, making them a powerful tool in the service of humanity. By mastering the art of healing through language, service providers can not only address immediate needs but also contribute to the long-term health and vitality of those they serve, proving that sometimes, the simplest of words can indeed be the most powerful of medicines.

*"The ethics of aid require us to think critically about the impact of our help; true assistance is that which empowers, rather than creates dependency."*

♡♡♡

# FIFTEEN

# THE ETHICS OF HELP: NAVIGATING THE COMPLEXITIES OF AID

The act of providing help, though ostensibly benevolent, is fraught with ethical complexities that can challenge the intentions and outcomes of such endeavors. Whether it involves humanitarian assistance, charitable donations, or interpersonal aid, navigating the ethics of help requires a thoughtful consideration of the consequences, motivations, and methods of assistance. This essay delves into the intricate landscape of providing help, highlighting the need for an ethical framework that ensures aid is both effective and respectful of the dignity and autonomy of those receiving it.

**Understanding the Need for Ethical Help**

At its core, the principle of helping is grounded in the desire to improve the well-being of others. However, without a careful ethical consideration, aid can sometimes lead to dependency, undermine local structures, or even exacerbate the problems it aims to solve.

The ethics of help, therefore, involves a careful balance between providing necessary support and fostering independence among aid recipients.

**Respecting Autonomy and Agency**

One of the fundamental ethical concerns in providing help is respecting the autonomy and agency of those being assisted. This means recognizing individuals as active agents in their own lives, capable of making decisions and taking actions to improve their situations. It challenges the paternalistic approach often seen in traditional aid models, where decisions are made on behalf of recipients without their input or consent. Instead, ethical help involves collaboration with beneficiaries to ensure that aid not only meets their immediate needs but also empowers them to lead their recovery or development.

**Avoiding Harm**

The ethical maxim "do no harm" is particularly pertinent in the context of aid. This principle requires that actions taken to help others should not inadvertently cause harm. For instance, aid should not distort local markets, displace local workers, or foster conflicts within communities. Understanding the local context and potential repercussions of aid is crucial to avoid such pitfalls. This might involve extensive field research, engagement with local leaders, and continuous monitoring and evaluation of aid impacts.

**Cultural Sensitivity**

Aid efforts must also be culturally sensitive. What is considered helpful or appropriate in one cultural context may not be in another. Ethical help respects and adapts to local customs, traditions, and social norms. It involves engaging with the community to understand these nuances and designing aid programs that are culturally congruent. Ignoring cultural aspects can lead to resistance, misunderstandings, and the failure of aid programs.

### Transparency and Accountability

Transparency and accountability in aid provision are critical to maintaining trust and ensuring that resources are used effectively. Donors, NGOs, and aid organizations must clearly communicate their goals, processes, and outcomes to both their beneficiaries and their sponsors. This openness helps to prevent corruption, mismanagement, and the misallocation of resources. It also allows stakeholders to hold organizations accountable for their actions, ensuring that aid reaches those who need it most.

### Building Sustainability

For aid to be ethically sound, it must aim for sustainability. This means that aid should not be a temporary fix but should contribute to creating lasting solutions that address the root causes of need. Sustainability involves building local capacity, supporting infrastructure development, and ensuring that projects are environmentally sustainable and economically viable over the long term.

### Motivations Behind Giving

The motivations for providing help should also be scrutinized. Ethical aid is given with the genuine intention of improving the lives of others, not for personal gain, political influence, or public relations benefits. When aid is given for the wrong reasons, it can lead to skewed priorities and ineffective assistance that serves the giver more than the receiver.

**Inclusive Decision-Making**

Inclusive decision-making is essential for ethical help. This involves including beneficiaries in the planning, implementation, and evaluation phases of aid projects. By doing so, aid providers can ensure that programs are relevant and effectively address the specific needs of the community. Inclusion also promotes ownership and engagement among recipients, which are key to the success and sustainability of aid efforts.

Navigating the complexities of aid requires a robust ethical framework that emphasizes respect for autonomy, cultural sensitivity, transparency, and sustainability. By adhering to these principles, individuals and organizations can provide help that not only addresses immediate needs but also promotes long-term development and empowerment. Ultimately, ethical help is about more than just providing resources; it is about supporting individuals and communities in a manner that respects their dignity, enhances their capacities, and contributes to a just and equitable world.

*"Celebrating service is celebrating humanity; it's acknowledging that beneath our diverse exteriors lies a shared desire to support, uplift, and unite."*

# SIXTEEN

# SERVICE ACROSS CULTURES: RESPECTING DIFFERENCES WHILE HELPING

In a globalized world, service initiatives often span across diverse cultures, necessitating a sensitive and informed approach to ensure effectiveness and respect. Engaging in service across different cultural landscapes presents unique challenges and opportunities that require an understanding of cultural norms, values, and expectations. This essay explores how service providers can navigate cultural diversity to deliver help that is both respectful and impactful, fostering positive relationships and sustainable outcomes.

**Cultural Competence in Service**

The foundation of successful cross-cultural service lies in cultural competence, which involves understanding and appropriately responding to the unique combination of cultural variables and the full range of human diversity. Cultural competence extends beyond awareness of cultural differences—it requires active steps to increase one's cultural knowledge and the ability to adapt services to meet culturally unique needs.

Service providers must first engage in a process of self-awareness and education to recognize their own cultural biases and perspectives. This self-examination is crucial as it prevents the imposition of one's cultural norms on others, which can lead to misunderstandings and reduce the effectiveness of aid. Education in this context involves learning about the cultural, social, economic, and political contexts of the communities served. It includes understanding local customs, languages, non-verbal communication cues, and the historical factors that have shaped these communities.

**Listening and Learning from the Community**

Effective service across cultures requires a listening approach where the voices and opinions of local community members are not only heard but also prioritized. This involves regular interaction with community members through focus groups, community meetings, and one-on-one conversations. Such engagements should be seen as learning opportunities for service providers to gain insights into the community's needs, desires, and the potential unintended consequences of proposed interventions.

By actively involving community members in the planning and implementation phases of service projects, providers ensure that the services are culturally appropriate and more likely to be accepted and sustained by the community. This participatory approach empowers communities, giving them a sense of ownership over projects and initiatives, which is critical for long-term success.

### Adapting Service Methods to Cultural Contexts

Adaptation involves tailoring service methods to fit the cultural contexts of the communities served. This may require modifications to communication styles, service delivery methods, and even the types of services provided. For instance, educational programs in areas with high illiteracy rates might rely more on visual aids and oral teachings rather than written materials. Health initiatives might need to consider local beliefs and practices around medicine and healing when designing treatment plans.

Furthermore, adaptation also involves timing and logistics. Understanding cultural concepts of time, significant cultural or religious dates, and local holidays are important for scheduling and implementing service activities in a way that respects the community's rhythms and norms.

### Building Trust and Fostering Respect

Trust is a crucial element in cross-cultural service. Building trust involves consistent, respectful interactions that demonstrate reliability and a genuine interest in the well-being of the community. This can be facilitated by employing local staff, engaging local leaders, and using local resources, which not only boosts the local economy but also shows respect for the community's capabilities.

Respect for the community also involves acknowledging and valuing the existing strengths and resources of the community. Every community has its assets, such as local knowledge, traditional practices, and community networks that can be pivotal in designing effective and sustainable service interventions.

### Addressing Language Barriers

Language differences can be a significant barrier in providing effective service across cultures. Employing bilingual staff, using professional translators, or providing language training for service providers are ways to overcome these barriers. Ensuring that communication is clear, respectful, and accessible helps in building understanding and facilitates more effective service delivery.

### Evaluating Impact and Gathering Feedback

Continuous evaluation and feedback are essential to ensure that cross-cultural services are effective and meet the needs of the community. This involves setting up feedback mechanisms through which community members can express their satisfaction or concerns regarding the services provided. Evaluations should consider cultural perspectives on what constitutes success and should respect the community's views and preferences.

Service across cultures is a complex yet rewarding endeavor that requires a deep commitment to understanding and respecting cultural diversity. By developing cultural competence, engaging in active listening, adapting services to local contexts, and building trust, service providers can deliver help that is not only effective but also dignified and respectful. Through such thoughtful and informed approaches, service initiatives can contribute to positive and lasting impacts in diverse communities around the world, fostering a global spirit of cooperation and respect.

*"The ripple effect of a single act of kindness can be monumental; never underestimate the power of small gestures to alter the course of another's life."*

ღღღ

# SEVENTEEN

# Technology for Good: Leveraging Tools for Better Outreach

In an era where technology permeates every aspect of life, its application in social service and humanitarian efforts presents a transformative opportunity. The concept of using technology for good encapsulates the integration of digital tools, platforms, and systems to enhance the efficiency and impact of service initiatives. This integration aids in scaling solutions, reaching underserved populations, and improving the delivery of aid and resources. This essay explores the multifaceted role of technology in expanding the reach and effectiveness of service efforts, examining both the potential benefits and the considerations necessary to ensure these tools foster genuine improvement in people's lives.

**Broadening Access through Digital Platforms**

One of the primary advantages of technology in service is its ability to overcome geographical barriers. Digital platforms can connect experts and resources to remote or underserved areas that traditionally lack access to quality education, healthcare, and other critical services. For instance, telemedicine can deliver expert medical consultations to rural clinics, while educational apps and online courses provide learning opportunities to students in remote regions. These technologies not only broaden access but also ensure continuity of service in challenging environments.

**Enhancing Communication and Coordination**

Technology improves communication channels between service providers and the communities they serve, as well as among the providers themselves. For example, mobile apps and social media platforms enable real-time interaction, making it easier to disseminate information, gather feedback, and engage with beneficiaries actively. For organizations, cloud-based tools and collaboration software can enhance internal operations and coordination, ensuring that teams spread across various locations can work seamlessly together, share data effectively, and align their efforts.

**Data-Driven Decision Making**

The capacity to collect, analyze, and utilize large volumes of data is another significant advantage offered by technology. Big data analytics can reveal patterns, trends, and insights that inform more effective planning and decision-making in service delivery. For instance, data analysis can help identify the most pressing needs within a community, optimize resource allocation, or evaluate the impact of current service programs. Moreover, technologies like geographic information systems (GIS) can be used to map crisis areas or plan the locations of new service facilities to maximize accessibility and impact.

## Increasing Transparency and Accountability

Technology also plays a crucial role in enhancing transparency and accountability in service endeavors. Blockchain technology, for example, can be used to track the flow of resources in aid distribution, ensuring that help reaches its intended recipients and reducing the risk of fraud or mismanagement. Similarly, online platforms that allow donors to see exactly how their contributions are being used can increase trust and encourage further participation and support from the public and funding bodies.

## Personalization of Services

Artificial intelligence (AI) and machine learning offer the potential to personalize services to meet individual needs more closely. In education, AI can adapt learning experiences to the pace and learning style of each student. In health services, AI can help personalize treatment plans based on a patient's unique health profile and history. Such personalized approaches not only improve outcomes but also enhance user engagement and satisfaction.

## Challenges and Ethical Considerations

While the benefits of technology for good are vast, there are significant challenges and ethical considerations that must be addressed. The digital divide—the gap between those who have access to modern information and communication technology and those who do not—can exacerbate existing inequalities if not carefully managed. Ensuring equitable access to the technology itself is therefore a fundamental prerequisite for these tools to be genuinely transformative.

Privacy and security are other major concerns, especially as service providers handle increasingly sensitive data. Protecting this data against breaches and ensuring it is used ethically and responsibly is critical to maintaining the trust of those being served.

Moreover, there is a risk of dependency on technology, which could undermine local capacities if technology solutions are not integrated thoughtfully. It is crucial that technology supports and enhances local systems rather than replacing them, ensuring sustainability and resilience within communities.

As we look to the future, the potential of technology to amplify the reach and impact of service efforts is boundless. However, leveraging technology for good requires more than just the deployment of tools; it requires a strategic and thoughtful approach that considers the social, economic, and cultural contexts in which these technologies operate. By navigating these challenges responsibly, service providers can harness the power of technology to create more inclusive, efficient, and effective solutions, truly leveraging these tools for the betterment of society.

*"Service is the mirror in which we see our true selves reflected; it reveals our capacity for kindness, our potential for impact, and our intrinsic connection to others."*

♡♡♡

# EIGHTEEN

# CELEBRATING SUCCESSES: RECOGNIZING ACHIEVEMENTS IN SERVICE

Celebrating successes and recognizing achievements in the realm of service is crucial not only for motivating those involved but also for fostering a culture of appreciation and positive reinforcement. Such recognition serves to highlight the impact of efforts made by individuals and organizations dedicated to helping others, which in turn can inspire continued work and greater involvement from the community. This essay explores the importance of celebrating successes in service, the different methods to effectively recognize contributions, and the profound impacts these practices can have on participants, beneficiaries, and the broader community.

## Importance of Recognizing Service Achievements

Recognizing achievements in service acts as a powerful motivator. It reaffirms to those involved that their efforts are valued and impactful, which is essential for maintaining morale and commitment. This is particularly significant in fields where the results of one's work may not be immediately visible, such as in social work, education, or long-term community development projects. Recognition helps to sustain motivation and enthusiasm, even through challenging or routine periods.

Furthermore, celebrating successes builds a narrative of positive change that can attract more attention and resources to a cause. Public recognition of the effective work being done can enhance an organization's reputation, which in turn can lead to increased funding, more volunteers, and broader community support. It also provides tangible examples of what can be achieved, serving as a powerful tool for advocacy and influence.

## Methods of Recognizing Achievements

There are numerous ways to recognize and celebrate successes in service, each with its unique impact and suitability depending on the context. Formal awards ceremonies are one popular method. These events can provide a platform to honor individuals or teams who have demonstrated outstanding commitment and achieved significant results. Such ceremonies not only reward the recipients but also serve as public endorsements of their efforts, which can enhance their credibility and visibility.

Informal recognition practices, such as highlighting achievements during team meetings, in organizational newsletters, or on social media, can also be very effective. These gestures, while smaller in scale, can foster a continuous and immediate culture of appreciation that keeps individuals and teams feeling valued and connected to the mission of their work.

Peer recognition programs are another impactful method. Allowing colleagues to nominate each other for awards or acknowledgments can enhance team cohesion and empower employees at all levels to partake in the culture of recognition. Peer recognition often carries a special significance as it comes directly from colleagues who witness the day-to-day dedication and hard work of their peers.

**Impacts of Celebrating Successes**

Celebrating successes has a profound impact on the individuals involved in service. It can significantly boost self-esteem and job satisfaction, leading to higher retention rates among volunteers and staff. It also encourages a healthy competition and a drive for excellence within organizations, as individuals and teams are inspired to strive for the standards of excellence they see being celebrated.

For the beneficiaries of service projects, seeing the successes of programs they are involved in can reinforce a sense of progress and hope. It can strengthen their engagement with the program and enhance their trust in the organization, which is crucial for the success of many community-based projects.

Broader community impacts include heightened visibility of important social issues and increased public engagement. When successes are celebrated and shared, they can educate the public about ongoing challenges and how they are being effectively addressed. This not only raises awareness but can also mobilize additional community support and involvement.

**Challenges in Recognizing Achievements**

While recognizing achievements is largely beneficial, it comes with its challenges. One risk is the potential for creating competitive or envious dynamics within organizations if not handled carefully. Ensuring that recognition practices are fair, transparent, and aligned with the values of the organization can mitigate these risks.

Another challenge is ensuring that the methods of recognition are culturally sensitive and appropriate, considering the diverse backgrounds of those involved in service. What may be regarded as rewarding in one culture could be seen as less appropriate in another.

Celebrating successes and recognizing achievements in service is essential for sustaining motivation, attracting support, and enhancing the effectiveness of service endeavors. By acknowledging the hard work and dedication of those involved in service, organizations not only reward past achievements but also pave the way for future successes. As such, developing a robust system of recognition should be a key component of any service organization's strategy, underpinning its efforts to foster a supportive and motivating environment. Through thoughtful and inclusive recognition practices, the true value of service can be celebrated, encouraging a continued commitment to making a positive impact in the lives of others.

*"Adapting our methods of service is a reflection of our respect for those we help; it acknowledges their changing needs and our commitment to meet them."*

♡♡♡

# NINETEEN

# REFLECTIONS ON SERVICE: PERSONAL STORIES OF TRANSFORMATION

Service, in its myriad forms, offers a profound avenue for personal and communal transformation. Often, the act of serving goes beyond the immediate impact of the aid provided, influencing the lives of those who give just as much as those who receive. Through personal stories of transformation, we can explore how service reshapes perspectives, builds unexpected bridges, and fosters deep, meaningful changes in individuals and communities. These narratives not only celebrate the victories and challenges of service but also provide insights into the rich, complex tapestry of human relationships that form when individuals commit to helping others.

**Personal Growth Through Service**

Service is a powerful catalyst for personal growth. Engaging in acts of service exposes individuals to new perspectives and challenges, pushing them to grow in ways they might not have anticipated.

Many find that through service, their understanding of the world expands—they become more aware of the struggles and hardships of others, as well as the resilience and strength that people exhibit in the face of adversity. This newfound awareness often leads to a deeper sense of empathy and a stronger commitment to ethical living.

For example, consider the story of a young volunteer who decided to spend a summer working with a community development organization in a rural area. Initially motivated by a vague desire to help, the volunteer faced the harsh realities of poverty, educational barriers, and systemic neglect firsthand. These experiences were emotionally challenging but transformative. The volunteer learned to navigate cultural differences, communicate effectively across barriers, and most importantly, to listen deeply to the community members, understanding their needs and aspirations. This experience fundamentally changed their outlook on life, steering them toward a career in social justice.

**Building Community Connections**

Service also plays a crucial role in building and strengthening community connections. When individuals come together to address communal challenges, they lay the groundwork for stronger, more cohesive communities. These connections are often sustained beyond the initial context of service, leading to lasting bonds and ongoing collaborative efforts.

A poignant example of this is seen in the aftermath of natural disasters when community members and external volunteers work side by side to rebuild and rehabilitate affected areas. In these scenarios, the act of service becomes a shared mission, transcending individual differences and fostering a collective identity. Years later, participants often reflect on these experiences as pivotal moments that reshaped their community's fabric and their role within it.

## Challenges and Overcoming Adversity

Service is not without its challenges, and these too are part of the transformational journey. Dealing with bureaucratic hurdles, facing resource constraints, and managing interpersonal conflicts are common challenges that can test the resolve and commitment of those involved in service. Overcoming these challenges often requires creativity, persistence, and resilience—qualities that are honed through the trials faced during service.

For instance, a volunteer teacher in an underfunded school might struggle with large class sizes and limited educational materials. The challenge of providing quality education under such circumstances can be daunting. However, through innovative teaching strategies, community involvement, and relentless advocacy for better resources, the teacher can make significant strides. This journey not only transforms the educational experiences of the students but also the teacher's skills and approach to teaching and advocacy.

## The Ripple Effect of Service

The impact of service often extends beyond the immediate context, creating a ripple effect that influences wider circles. Volunteers and service workers carry the lessons and insights gained from their experiences into other areas of their lives, influencing their families, workplaces, and communities.

For example, a corporate executive who volunteers at a homeless shelter might bring back insights about the complex causes of homelessness to their professional life, advocating for corporate policies that support affordable housing or job training for vulnerable populations. This transfer of insights and advocacy can amplify the impact of their initial service, leading to broader societal changes.

Reflections on service and personal stories of transformation illuminate the profound and varied impacts of service on individuals and communities. These narratives underscore the power of service to teach, challenge, and connect us in deep and enduring ways. They remind us that service is not just an act of giving but a mutual exchange that enriches everyone involved, weaving a dense fabric of empathy, understanding, and commitment that can sustain communities through times of need and times of abundance. By sharing and celebrating these stories, we not only honor those who serve but also inspire others to engage in acts of service, perpetuating a cycle of positive change and mutual growth.

*"The legacy of service is written in the stories of those whose lives have been touched; these narratives are the true measures of our impact and success."*

ᐅᐅᐅ

# TWENTY

# Looking Forward: How to Keep the Spirit of Service Alive

In a world increasingly characterized by individualism and division, the spirit of service stands as a beacon of collective action and mutual support. Keeping the spirit of service alive is essential not only for addressing the myriad social, environmental, and economic challenges facing communities but also for fostering a sense of connectedness and humanity among people. This essay explores various strategies to ensure that the spirit of service continues to thrive and expand, influencing generations to come.

**Cultivating a Culture of Service**

The foundation of sustaining a spirit of service lies in cultivating a culture that values and prioritizes these efforts. This involves embedding service-oriented values in the fabric of communities, from schools and workplaces to governments and non-profit organizations. Education systems play a critical role in this process by integrating service learning into their curricula. When children and young adults engage in community service as part of their education, they develop a natural inclination towards helping others, which can last a lifetime.

Workplaces can also foster a spirit of service by encouraging and facilitating volunteerism among employees. Companies can offer paid leave for volunteer activities or organize corporate social responsibility (CSR) initiatives that involve staff in ongoing service projects. Such practices not only contribute to the community but also build team cohesion and employee morale, demonstrating that service is valued within the corporate culture.

**Leveraging Technology**

Technology offers powerful tools to keep the spirit of service alive by enhancing the reach and impact of service activities. Digital platforms can connect volunteers with opportunities that match their skills and interests and can facilitate virtual volunteering, allowing individuals to contribute regardless of geographical constraints. Social media can amplify the stories of service and its impacts, inspiring others to take action. Additionally, technology can streamline the administrative aspects of organizing volunteer activities, making it easier for organizations to manage projects and for individuals to participate.

**Recognizing and Celebrating Volunteers**

Recognition is a key factor in motivating continued involvement in service activities. Regular acknowledgment of volunteers' efforts—whether through awards, public acknowledgment, or simple thank-you notes—can significantly boost morale and encourage ongoing commitment. Celebrations and recognition events also serve to raise awareness about the value of service and can inspire others to start their service journeys.

**Building Community Partnerships**

Sustaining the spirit of service requires a collaborative approach. Partnerships between different sectors—public, private, and non-profit—can pool resources and expertise to tackle larger projects and reach wider audiences. These collaborations can take various forms, such as joint ventures, sponsorships, or support networks, and help to weave a dense fabric of service across community lines.

**Adapting to Changing Needs**

The spirit of service is dynamic and must adapt to the evolving challenges and needs of society. Organizations and individuals engaged in service must stay informed about the issues facing their communities and the world at large. Being responsive to change ensures that service activities remain relevant and effective, addressing real and immediate needs rather than adhering to outdated models.

**Fostering Leadership and Sustainability**

Developing future leaders who are committed to service is essential for keeping the spirit of service alive. This involves mentoring young people and providing them with leadership opportunities within service projects. Sustainability also means ensuring that projects are designed to have a lasting impact and do not depend solely on continuous external support. Building local capacity and ensuring community ownership of projects can help achieve this sustainability.

**Incorporating Inclusivity**

Service must be inclusive, providing opportunities for all individuals to contribute, regardless of age, background, ability, or socioeconomic status. Inclusive service practices ensure that everyone can participate in and benefit from service activities, strengthening the collective spirit of the community.

**Encouraging Reflection and Feedback**

Reflection is a crucial aspect of service that allows individuals and organizations to understand the impact of their actions, learn from their experiences, and make necessary adjustments. Feedback from those served and those serving provides valuable insights that can enhance the effectiveness and relevance of service initiatives.

Keeping the spirit of service alive is a multifaceted endeavor that requires intention, innovation, and community collaboration. By cultivating a culture of service, leveraging technology, recognizing contributions, building partnerships, adapting to changes, fostering leadership, promoting inclusivity, and encouraging reflection, communities can ensure that the spirit of service not only endures but flourishes. These efforts create a legacy of service that inspires future generations to commit themselves to the betterment of society, perpetuating a cycle of goodwill and transformative impact.

*"Keeping the spirit of service alive requires a heart that never hardens, a touch that never hurts, and a generosity that never seeks to gain."*

# TWENTY-ONE
# SUMMARY

In an exploration of the multifaceted nature of service and its profound impact on both individuals and communities, we delved into various aspects of service—from its ethical considerations to the leveraging of technology, and from personal transformation stories to the importance of maintaining a spirit of service. This comprehensive examination reveals that service is not merely an act of giving but a complex interaction that fosters growth, understanding, and change in myriad ways. Here, we summarize the key insights and overarching themes from the detailed discussions on the different facets of service.

**1. The Foundations of Service**

Service is built on a commitment to enhancing the welfare of others. It requires an understanding of the needs and circumstances of those being served and a willingness to act selflessly. The foundational aspects of service, such as empathy, respect, and compassion, are critical in ensuring that service efforts are both effective and humane. These values not only guide direct interactions with beneficiaries but also influence the planning and execution of service projects.

### 2. Personal and Community Transformation

Service has a dual impact—it transforms both the provider and the receiver. Volunteers and service workers often experience significant personal growth, gaining new perspectives and developing a deeper understanding of societal issues. For recipients, service can provide essential resources, support, and opportunities that catalyze significant improvements in their quality of life. Community-wide, service builds resilience, strengthens ties, and fosters a cooperative spirit, enhancing the collective capacity to face future challenges.

### 3. Ethical Considerations in Service

Providing help comes with complex ethical considerations, including ensuring respect for the autonomy and dignity of those helped, avoiding unintended harm, and understanding cultural nuances. Ethical service is about more than just doing good—it's about doing good well and responsibly. It requires continuous reflection, learning, and adaptation to ensure that service actions are both morally sound and effective.

### 4. Technology as an Enabler

Technology has transformed service delivery, enabling broader reach and more efficient operations. From digital platforms that connect volunteers with opportunities to data analytics that inform more strategic decision-making, technology can significantly amplify the impact of service efforts. However, it also introduces challenges such as the digital divide and privacy concerns, which must be managed carefully to truly harness technology for good.

### 5. Recognizing and Celebrating Service

Recognition plays a vital role in sustaining the spirit of service. Celebrating successes and acknowledging the contributions of volunteers and organizations motivate continued effort and signal to the broader community the value of service. Recognition can take many forms, from formal awards to informal acknowledgments in social media or community gatherings.

### 6. Building Sustainable Service Models

Sustainability in service is crucial for ensuring long-term impact. This involves creating initiatives that are not only effective in the short term but also viable in the long term. Sustainable service requires planning for the future, investing in community capacity building, and ensuring that projects are environmentally responsible and culturally appropriate.

### 7. Challenges in Service

Service work is not without its challenges, including resource limitations, burnout among volunteers, and the complexities of addressing deeply entrenched societal problems. Overcoming these challenges requires resilience, creativity, and a commitment to continuous improvement and innovation in service methods.

### 8. Future Directions in Service

Looking forward, keeping the spirit of service alive will involve adapting to changing societal needs, embracing new technologies, and fostering a global culture of service. It will also require nurturing the next generation of service leaders, expanding inclusivity in service opportunities, and continually enhancing the ethical frameworks that guide service efforts.

Service is a dynamic and evolving field that touches every aspect of human life. It is bound by the common threads of empathy, commitment, and transformation. By understanding the complexities and embracing the challenges associated with service, individuals and organizations can contribute to a more just, compassionate, and resilient world. Through collective effort and shared responsibility, the spirit of service can continue to thrive, driving positive change across communities and generations.

# Citation And References

This book represents the culmination of extensive research and meticulous analysis, incorporating a diverse range of sources, including numerous books, scholarly studies, and personal experiences. Additionally, I have scoured various websites to gather relevant information and data essential for the compilation of this work. I have taken every precaution to ensure the accuracy of the information presented and have diligently cited all sources to acknowledge their contributions.

Despite these efforts, the possibility of inadvertent errors remains. I deeply value the insights of my readers and appreciate any feedback that can help identify and rectify such inaccuracies. I encourage you to bring any discrepancies to my attention.

Your feedback is not only welcome but crucial, as it will aid in correcting current editions and enhancing the content of future ones. I am committed to maintaining the highest standards of accuracy and reliability in my work and thank you for your support and understanding.

Additionally, I firmly uphold the principle of freedom of speech and expression as guaranteed under Article 19(1)(a) of the Constitution of India, and I respect the diverse viewpoints and expressions of all readers.

# Other Books Of The Author

1. Empowering Minds: A Journey into Women's Self-Discovery and Power
2. The Dynamics of Motivation: Catalyzing Thought into Action
3. Meditation and Mental Well Being: The Path to Inner Peace and Clarity
4. The Psychology of Child Education: Nurturing Future Generations
5. Ethical Enlightenment: A Modern Guide to Living with Integrity
6. Voices of Empowerment: Stories of Women Rising Against Odds
7. Social Psychology in Everyday Life: Understanding Human Connections
8. The Essence of Motivational Speaking: Inspiring Change in Others
9. Balancing Acts: Women, Work, and the Will to Lead
10. Guiding with Grace: Raising Children with Compassion and Awareness
11. The Power of Positive Aging: Embracing Life After Fifty
12. Building Resilient Communities: Social Work in Action
13. The Ethical Educator: Principles for Teaching and Learning
14. From Insight to Impact: Social Psychology for a Better World
15. The Ethics of Empathy: A Guide to Ethical Living
16. The Science of Empowering the Self: Navigating Life's Challenges with Psychological Wisdom
17. The Mindful Conscious Leader: Meditation Techniques for Modern Management
18. Pioneering Spirit: Women's Pathways to Leadership and Empowerment
19. Feeling to Healing: The Role of Emotional Intelligence in Child Development
20. Transformative Talks and Words of Inspiration: Insights into Motivational Oratory

21. Green Ethics: A Path to Sustainable Living
22. Spiritual Integrity: Navigating Life with Moral Compassion
23. Clean Living, Clean Society: The Ethics of Cleanliness
24. Patriotic Spirits: Building a Nation on Positive Attitudes
25. Innovative Integrity & Vibrant Visions: The Ethical and Entrepreneurial Spirit of Gujarat
26. Youthful Visions, Endless Possibilities: Inspiring Ethics and Motivation in Children
27. Living Your Legacy: How to Motivate Others by Living Your Values
28. Secret of Healing Conversations: Ethical Practices in Counselling and Therapy
29. Creative Kindness: Crafting a Life of Compassion and Creativity
30. The Power of Appreciation: How Gratitude Can Transform Your Relationships
31. Bhagavad-Gita: Messages
32. Science of Art: The New Frontier of Fashion Modernism
33. Vivekananda's Virtues: A Blueprint for Modern Living
34. Empower Her: Navigating the Path to Women's Entrepreneurship
35. The Boundless Classroom: Innovations in Global Education
36. The Language of Leadership: Communicating with Authenticity and Impact
37. The Warrior's Mantra: Deciphering the Hanuman Chalisa
38. Echoes of Empathy: Transformative Stories of Social Service
39. Artful Living: Cultivating Creativity in Your Daily Routine
40. Finding Your Why: Discovering Your Passions and Charting Your Course
41. The Role of Social Media in Shaping Self-Esteem and Interpersonal Relationships among Adolescents
42. Karma's Tapestry: Weaving a Life of Selfless Service
43. Altruistic Alchemy: Transforming Lives Through Giving
44. The Blueprint of Pro-Activeness and Productivity: Crafting Habits for Success
45. The Simplicity with Grounded Wisdom: Embracing Authenticity

in a Complex World

46. Secret of Solopreneur's Odyssey: Navigating the Path to Self-Employment
47. Exploring Tapestry of Peace: Global Perspectives on Harmony
48. The Art and Actions of Connection: Mastering Communication for Impact
49. She Governs and at the Helm: Strategies for Political Empowerment
50. Rising Above and Rising with Grace: A Woman's Roadmap to Career Mastery
51. The Effect of Networking & Connectedness: Building Strategic Alliances for Women
52. Beyond his Barriers: Women Thriving in Male-Dominated Fields
53. Secret of Inner Compass: Navigating Life with Intuition
54. Creative & Pro-Active Muses: A Celebration of Women in the Arts
55. Unburdened: The Art of Releasing the Past
56. Amplified Voices: Speeches of Women that Astonished the World
57. Secret of Manifesting Dreams: A Woman's Guide to Intentional Living
58. Ethics and Value Based Education: Reimagining Japan's School System
59. The Moral Compass Curriculum: A Holistic Approach
60. Tech with Heart: Integrating Ethics into Digital Learning
61. Honoring Virtue: Recognizing Ethical Excellence in Education
62. Raising Good Humans: A Guide to Character Development
63. The Spark Within: Nurturing Creativity in Children
64. The Teenager Whisperer: Navigating Adolescence with Grace
65. Igniting a Passion for Learning: Inspiring Lifelong Curiosity
66. The Habit Lab: Cultivating Positive Behaviors in Children
67. Seeds of Empathy: Fostering Compassion in Young Hearts
68. The Reading Revolution: Inspiring a Love of Books in Children
69. The Learning Brain: Unlocking the Secrets of Student Success
70. Teaching for All: Differentiated Instruction Strategies
71. The Time Alchemist: Mastering Time Management for Peak Performance

72. The Resilience Factor: Transforming Setbacks into Stepping Stones
73. The Healing Touch of Nature: An Introduction to Naturopathy
74. Echoes of the Past: Healing Through Past Life Regression
75. The Spiritual Healer's Handbook: Exploring Energy Medicine
76. Crystal Clarity: Unveiling the Power of Gemstones
77. The Dream Weaver's Guide: Decoding the Language of Dreams
78. Emotional Alchemy: Transforming Pain into Power
79. Sonic Serenity: Harnessing Sound for Stress Relief
80. The Entrepreneur's Playbook: Launching Your Business with Confidence
81. Productivity Unleashed: Time Management Strategies for Entrepreneurs
82. The Problem Solver's Toolkit: Creative Solutions for Business Challenges
83. The Future is Now: Emerging Trends in Business
84. The Curious Explorer: A Child's Guide to Scientific Discovery
85. Digital Pioneers: Empowering Kids in the Tech World
86. The Young Philosopher's Guide: Exploring Life's Big Questions
87. Finding Your Voice: Communication Skills for Confident Kids
88. Nature's Playground: A Child's Guide to Outdoor Adventure
89. Growing a Greener Tomorrow: A Guide to Tree Planting & Conservation
90. Driving with Purpose: Ethical Choices on the Road
91. The Healing Touch: Cultivating Compassion in Healthcare
92. Navigating the Digital Landscape: Ethics in the Age of Social Media
93. The Ethical Closet: A Guide to Sustainable Fashion
94. The Mindful Voyager: Sustainable Travel Practices
95. The Feminine Divine: Honoring the Goddesses of India
96. Sacred Sounds: Chanting Your Way to Inner Peace
97. The Yoga Path: Uniting with the Divine Within
98. Rites of Passage: Creating Meaningful Ceremonies
99. The Chakra System: A Map of Inner Transformation
100. Spiritual Sangha: Finding Community through Satsang and

Bhajan
101. Pilgrimage of the Soul: Spiritual Journeys in India

# Contact

Dr. Minakshi Bansal
Social Activist
Ahmedabad, Gujarat, Bharat
minakshiindiag20@yahoo.com

|| LOKAHA SAMASTHAHA SUKHINO BHAVANTU ||

www.ingramcontent.com/pod-product-compliance
Lightning Source LLC
LaVergne TN
LVHW042351150826
845671LV00002B/87

* 9 7 9 8 8 9 4 4 6 1 9 1 5 *